Copyright © 2021 The Recruit

Email address: lavell@crossandcrownconsulting.com

Published By: LaVell McCullers crossandcrownconsulting.com

TABLE OF CONTENTS

Instagram: @CROSSANDCROWNCONSULTING , @therecruitingmentor

Introduction

I'm so excited that you are reading my book! My goal is to teach student-athletes and parents how to navigate the recruiting process and earn scholarships. Too many times, I've seen student-athletes give up on their dream of playing sports collegiately, mainly because they don't have the proper guidance and information to help them navigate through. For the first time in book form, I am sharing everything you need to know about the recruiting process to make your dreams come true or help make your child's dreams come true. I followed these exact steps to make my own dream come true. With this information, I earned over 20+ scholarship offers and got to play on the Division 1 level. Now I am looking to share my knowledge to help other student-athletes reach their dreams.

Before we jump into strategies, I want to share a little about myself. I grew up in the small town of Havre de Grace, Maryland. l started my high school journey at Havre de Grace High School and ultimately ended it at Aberdeen High School. I played both football and basketball. Football was my favorite sport, so I chose to take that route to school. As a freshman, I started my first football game on Varsity playing quarterback because our star QB was out. Looking back on it, I was honestly scared to death. I didn't know any of the plays and I hadn't practiced with the team. It took my parent's and my brother's encouragement to convince me to even get on the bus. During that game, I threw for 3 touchdowns and we won. It just goes to show that having a little faith can go a long way. The next week our star QB returned.

Instead of sitting on the bench, I decided to play Junior Varsity to develop my skills. During that JV year, I put up some amazing numbers and I moved up to Varsity as a sophomore.

That off-season, our Varsity head coach left for another school, so my team got a new coaching staff. Our team didn't perform well that season but I started gaining interest from a few colleges, including Duke University. My dad took me on a visit to the school to meet the coaches and watch a game. The coaching staff told me they were coming to my high school that next Monday to talk to my coach. When I got home from school on Monday, my mom and dad had some horrible news. My parents told me that the coach from Duke had came to my school that day. He told my parents that they were coming to offer me a full scholarship, but after speaking with my new head coach they didn't think I was the right fit for their program. To this day, I still don't know what was said in that meeting. I was the star athlete at the school and a team-voted captain. I do know my coach was angry that I had planned to transfer to another school to gain more exposure from college coaches. This might have played a part in what he said to the Duke coaches. This was the first time in my life that I felt like giving up on my dream, but my mom always preached "We don't quit in this family." So I never gave up! I had faith that I could make my dream come true.

My father did everything he could to help me make my dream happen. He educated and coached me through the recruiting process. He got me a personal trainer. He spent many paychecks paying for me to go to camps. I know some people aren't as fortunate to have both parents in their life or even have parents who are financially stable. That's why I am writing this book to help guide them.

After a lot of hard work, prayer and faith, I went to Marist College, a Division 1 AA institution in New York. Although Marist was known for its outstanding academics, it wasn't what I was looking for athletically. I ended up redshirting and becoming unfocused, and because of my lack of focus I got in a little trouble and decided to leave the school. I had confidence that I could earn a full scholarship and play at a higher level so I took a leap of faith. I transferred to City College of San Francisco, a Junior College, 2500 miles away from home where I had to go through the recruiting process again, but this time I was on my own. I earned a full scholarship to Prairie View A&M University, a Division 1 AA school outside of Houston, Texas. You will learn more about the ups and downs I went through in my journey and how I used faith to overcome those obstacles throughout this book.

So what brings me here today? Why did I decide to write a book to teach student-athletes and parents how to navigate the recruiting process? Here's why:

Growing up my dream was to always play college ball. I started out playing running back and I can remember back to my childhood, waking up early in the morning to call my best friends and watch College Gameday. As I started through my middle school years, my brother was playing sports in high school. I can't recall many athletes going to college from our area. When I got to high school, I played with many talented athletes, but for some reason, things hadn't changed. I was one of only five athletes to go to school to play collegiately. This wasn't just on my football team, this was throughout our entire sports program. Honestly, if it wasn't for my Dad dedicating himself to learning the recruiting process and making sure he did everything in his power to get me to school, I don't think I would have gotten recruited. When I went to college, I frequently checked in on my hometown to see which athletes were going off to school. I found more of the same, not many student-athletes were going to college. This bothered me because we have some great talent in my area. I started to wonder why this was happening and why nobody was doing anything to change it.

After having a conversation with one of the athletes from my area. I found my answer. The person I was talking to was one of the best local athletes to never make it to college. We were reminiscing about our most memorable highlights, and that's when we started talking about all of the great athletes from our area who never made it out.

We recalled athletes whose grades held them back or others who were focused on being in the streets and several other reasons. I decided to ask what he thought held him back the most. I started by asking him about what he did to make sure that coaches knew who he was when he was in school. His answer was simple. He replied "nothing." Of course, knowing him for a while I already knew this answer but I wanted to dig a little deeper. I proceeded to ask him why he didn't put together a highlight tape and send it out to coaches just to introduce himself. His second answer was shocking to me, he stated "I thought my coaches were supposed to do that; I didn't even know I could contact coaches." This shocked me because when I was in high school this was something I knew I had to do. I also remembered that my dad had educated me on the recruiting process and helped me navigate through it.

That's when it hit me, not all student-athletes are educated on the recruiting process and most of them don't have the proper guidance that's going to get them to the next level. For some reason, the parents, the coaches, and the student- athletes from my area didn't have this crucial information. I dug a little deeper and found out that this was a problem in many towns all over the country. This is when I decided to combine my passion for helping others with my recruiting process knowledge and experiences to create my company and ultimately write this book. This book will serve as an instrumental guide that will help you navigate through the recruiting process and reach the next level. In this book, I share my knowledge, experience, and advice that I've gained throughout my journey to help guide you to your destination.

Without further ado, The Recruiting Compass.

COMMITMENT

If you are reading this page that means you are investing in yourself and I want to thank you for that. Before we get started I need your commitment. I don't want this book to be a book that you buy, read and then you don't apply the information you learned. Information can only change your situation if it is applied! I need you to commit to applying all of the information you learn while reading this book. I need you to commit to taking notes. Lastly, I want you to commit to having faith in yourself, in your support system, and also in God. I want you to write this statement down on a piece of paper. Once you are finished I want you to sign, date, and put it somewhere you can see it every day. The statement is:

"I am committed to applying the knowledge that I learn from this book into my life. I am committed to having faith. I understand that my success depends 100% on me taking action. I am committed to making my dreams come true!"

Signature: Date:

This statement is a promise to yourself to hold yourself accountable. This statement means you will do everything in your power to make your dreams come true. Once you complete this you are ready to take the next step!

Mentality

A major component of being successful in life is your mentality. Your mentality refers to your way of thinking and learning. The recruiting process is a long but enjoyable one. Both student-athletes and their parents have to be mentally tough in order to maximize their potential.

Parents - make sure your children know this will be a tough process and also make sure they understand that not all coaches will want to recruit them. The good thing about the recruiting process is there are approximately 5,300 colleges and universities in the US, and if you apply the information in this book, at least one of them will recruit you.

When it comes to mentality, I want to offer some advice. Make sure that you are always working to build a student mentality and build your integrity. This mentality adopts the idea that you are always willing to learn and take in new information. This makes you coachable and will take you a long way, in not just sports, but life in general. Be willing to take constructive criticism (which was something I struggled with early on in my career.) I wasn't able to understand why coaches were hard on me all the time. When I got older, I understood that most coaches have your best interest at heart. Coaches used to always say that once they stop yelling and pushing you, they don't care anymore.

I see so many coaches give up on athletes because they aren't coachable. You need to be willing to take in all the information that you can from them because they are only trying to help you become the best person possible. Be willing to learn – both in the classroom and the film room - to become better at your craft. When it comes to integrity, NFL Hall Of Fame Coach, Tony Dungy defined it as "the choice between what's convenient & what's right." When it comes to the recruiting process and life in general integrity can carry you a long way. During the recruiting process, referrals and recommendations are huge! You need to make sure that people don't hesitate to give you the referral or recommendation when coaches ask for athletes or ask about who you are as a person.

A lot of athletes overlook this aspect. They think that what they do outside of their sport or outside of school doesn't affect them. That couldn't be further from the truth. When I look back on my situation with Duke, I wasn't operating with integrity. Yes, I was a top athlete, but I was sleeping in class, I was talking back to my coaches, and I wasn't being the man I knew I could be. That is probably why Duke decided to pass on me. Make sure you are doing the right things even when you think no one is watching because I promise you someone is always watching.

The best way to make sure that you have your head on straight is to make sure you are being honest, setting goals, and having faith! Let's dive a little deeper.

HONESTY

In order to get to the next level, parents and their student-athletes have to be on the same page mentally. My father and I had to get on the same page about a few things when I was starting the recruiting process. I was a little stubborn, which led us to argue sometimes. I remember we argued because I wasn't being honest with my talent level and what division I wanted to play in. Like all athletes, I naturally wanted to play on the highest level which is division 1, in a POWER 5 conference. I wanted to go to the biggest school with the brightest lights but I wasn't honest with the situation I was in. I was playing at a very small high school that got little to no exposure. I had to ask myself these questions: "Was I good enough to play at the highest level?" "Did I just want to sit on the bench or did I want to go somewhere I could compete to play immediately?" and ultimately "was it possible to get to a POWER 5 school from the school I was attending?" I wasn't where I needed to be physically and I had to ask myself was willing to put the work in to make sure that I could reach that level. If I wasn't willing to put the work in, I would never have been successful then or now.

As parents and as student-athletes you don't want to get caught up reaching out to schools that are above your talent level. You will miss a lot of opportunities and waste time if you are not honest. For example, if you have the talent level of a Division 2 player but you are focused on going to a Division 1 school, you might be missing out on the Division 2 opportunities. That's why it is critical to get-evaluated by an expert. An expert could be a college coach, a recruiting coach like me, a personal trainer, or someone who you trust and has been there before. If you really want to get to the Division 1 level, it's possible, but you are going to have to sacrifice & commit to getting better at your craft. You are going to have to spend a lot of time getting bigger, faster, stronger, and smarter than your competition. Keep in mind that only 2- 3% of all athletes earn a Division 1 scholarship, and only half of them actually play once they get to that level. It is also important to note that if you have dreams of playing professionally you can still achieve those dreams by going to a smaller school. Shannon Sharpe, Hall of Famer, and regarded as the best tight end in NFL history came from Savannah State University, a smaller school in Georgia. Steph Curry, regarded as the best shooter in NBA history came from Davidson University, a smaller school.

As a student-athlete, you need to be honest with what you want for your future. This is important because it will influence everything you do on a daily basis. Your parents can only push you so hard. When I was getting ready to go to high school, I wanted to be in the mix with all of my friends so badly. I wanted to be a class clown, get in trouble, and all the typical things teenagers do. When I discovered that I could use my love for the game to get my education paid for, I started to take my future seriously. I can remember my father telling me I was going to have to change the people I hung around with if I wanted to be successful.

That statement remains true to this day. You are a product of the company you keep. What entertains you, trains you. If you want to be successful you have to hang around successful people or people who have the same goals in mind. This required me to detach myself from my friends sometimes and invest my time into my future. I'm not saying that they didn't want to be successful but they didn't want the same things I wanted for my future. I used that time to get in extra work on the field, go to camps, message, call, and email coaches, put extra hours into film study, and anything that was going to help me make my dreams come true. It got to a point where I was so worn out, I had to take a break. I couldn't have done it without my support system investing in my future and pushing me to be the best I could be. This leads me to my next point:

Parents - you have to be honest about how much you are willing to invest in your child's future. Once I told my dad I wanted to go to school and play college sports, he did everything in his power to make sure that it came true. So much so that my brother-in-law had to tell him to let me take a break sometimes. He only did this because he saw that I was committed to making it happen myself. I thank him for it because

without him it wouldn't be possible for me to be here today.

Parents - you want to make sure your child is committed to their own success before going all in. Once your child is committed to their own success, there are many ways to invest in their future. This could be putting them into different camps. These camps could be developmental camps to help them grow their skills or they could be combines and/or college camps. We will cover camps in more detail later on but camps allow athletes to compete against other competitors to get noticed and gain exposure from college coaches. You could also get your child a personal trainer to help them develop their skills. My dad also helped me by getting me professional guidance from someone who knew the recruiting process in & out. That expert helped guide me through the recruiting process, and also answer any questions that came about. There are many different ways to invest in your child's future. Pick the one that best suits them and be consistent. It has to be consistent to work.

SETTING GOALS

I want you to dream big! Then I want you to dream 10x bigger than that. I want you to think of all of the things you want to accomplish from now until you make it to your desired destination. Now write them down and put them somewhere you can see them every day. If you speak with any successful athlete, business owner, entrepreneur, or coach they will tell you that once you get honest, and you commit, you have to start setting goals.

Goals are milestones on your way to your big dream. Goals help you stay focused on the bigger picture. Goals can be as small or as big as you want them to be. Some examples could be making an A on your next test or wanting to make a million dollars. If you don't know where to start with goal setting start with your next test, or your next game. Write a small goal of how many touchdowns you want to score, or how many rebounds you want to grab, or even how many home runs you want to hit in that next game. This not only puts you in the mindset to succeed but also sets the path of doing everything possible to make sure you achieve those goals. Make sure you are writing your goals down, creating visual guides, and putting your goals somewhere you can see them every day! This serves as a reminder to keep pushing. You also want to make sure that you are creating goals for yourself. Not just in sports, but in life. We get caught up in what other individuals are doing or how fast that person got to their destination. You want to embrace your own path and your own journey. You are your own person and you are completely different from anyone else. Set goals with only yourself in mind.

Last but not least, I want to introduce you to something that Steve Harvey, one of the original Kings of Comedy and host of Family Feud, introduced to me. It is a popular goal-setting method called the SMART method. It stands for Specific, Measurable, Attainable, Relevant, and Time-Sensitive. Parents - this is something that you will have to do with your child. Here are some of the things you want to keep in mind as you go through setting

SMART GOALS:

Make the goals Specific - Create goals with your dreams in mind. They should be defined and clear on what you are trying to accomplish. Example: I want to score touchdowns.

How will you Measure your goal? - Now that you have your goal defined you want to be able to measure how you are doing. This means putting real dates, times, and amounts on your goals. If you need a push, ask someone to hold you accountable. Example: I want to score 3 touchdowns by the end of the next game.

Your goals should be Attainable - your goals should be something that you can reach but it should also require a challenge. You don't want your goals to be too easy. You won't maximize your full potential by creating goals that don't push you outside of your comfort zone. You will surprise yourself with how much you can achieve if you push yourself a little. Bad Example: I want to score one touchdown this season.

You want to create goals that are Real and Relevant - You want to create goals that align directly with your dreams and aspirations. You don't want goals that are going to have you running in circles and ultimately wasting your time.

Time-Sensitive - Your goals need to have a deadline. This will keep you focused on the tasks at hand. This will also help you map out what you need to be doing on your path to your dream. Example: I want to score 5 Touchdowns and have 200 yards rushing by game 5. I want to have 10 total touchdowns this season and 500 total rushing yards at the end of the season

FAITH

One of my favorite scriptures from the Bible is 2 Corinthians 5:7, "For we walk by faith, not by sight." You can apply this to any aspect of your life. There isn't a person out there who doesn't go through their own ups and downs. The downs are not what define us as athletes, and as people... it's what we do with those downs that define us.

Parents - make sure that your child knows that you believe in them, you have faith in them, and that you support their dreams. It is important that they know that you are there for them so that they don't give up.

One instance that stands out the most in my life, when we are talking about faith is a situation I went through in college. Like many student-athletes, I strived to make it to play sports professionally. Like we discussed earlier, I earned the right to attend Marist College out of high school. It was a great school academically, one of the top schools in the nation, but after a semester, I found out it wasn't what I was looking for athletically. I knew that I could play at a higher level so I decided to step out on faith and believe in myself. I decided to transfer schools. My first transfer was to Globe College in NYC. I ended up wasting a semester there because I found out that some of the credits weren't accredited and didn't transfer to other 4-year universities. I had a crucial choice to make, I could either give up on trying to get a scholarship and walk-on to Maryland University, or I could have faith in myself and take the Junior College route. I decided to take the latter route. I had already wasted so much time but I knew I had the talent to earn a full scholarship. I moved across the country to play for City College of San Francisco, one of the top Junior Colleges in the nation. I spent two years there and earned my Associates's Degree. We also won a Junior College National Football Championship. If you're not familiar with the junior college process you have to complete your AA degree or get a certain amount of credits to be able to earn a scholarship and transfer back to a 4-year university.

This route is the toughest route of them all and not a lot of people make it out of Junior College. I was going to school, working a full-time job, and playing football just to make my dream come true.

I had to share a one-bedroom apartment with 5 other athletes and we were all paying $750 a month each. Some of my teammates were taking the BART train 2 hours back and forth to school every day just to make a way for themselves. On top of that, I had to battle the politics of coaches picking favorites because of former family members going to the school. I never complained. I grinded it out and did what I had to do to come out on top. Things were rough but it was worth it for me in the end. It made the journey so much sweeter. Once I started balling out I had to go through the recruiting process again. This time when I went through the recruiting process I was by myself. I ended up earning over 20+ scholarship offers with the information I'm going to give you in this book.

I chose to attend Prairie View A&M University. I had a pretty good career at PVAMU, being able to achieve awards like Freshman Player of the Week, SWAC Newcomer of the Week, and others. Going into my senior year, I had professional scouts coming to watch my practice, and it felt like I was so close to making my dream come true but being a D1 quarterback I let the hype get to my head and I got "lost in the sauce." I was focused on females, parties, being cool, and not focused on getting better at my craft. Suddenly, things took a turn for the worse. I got into some trouble my senior year and due to some unfortunate circumstances, I wasn't able to finish out my college career. This was one of the lowest moments in my life. I felt like everything I had accomplished up to that point was for nothing. I felt I had let my parents, family, supporters, teammates, and coaches down again. I was in a bad place for a while. I didn't even want to finish school and I was ready to give up again. This was another time that I had to have faith. I had faith that God had a plan for me and that everything was happening for a reason. I also had faith that my support system was going to do everything they could to make sure that I finished.

I started to pray and ask God to show me the way. Slowly, I started to believe that everything was going to work out in my favor. Sure enough, I graduated on time from PVAMU with a 3.0 GPA and a Bachelor's Degree in Criminal Justice. I was also able to compete in my university's athletic pro day, where almost 30 NFL, XFL, and Arena Football League coaches were in attendance. I performed well at the pro day and although I didn't get drafted, I had conversations with the Browns and Rams coaches afterward. Again I was at a crossroads with what to do with my life.

I didn't get drafted and I didn't know where to go next with my life. I was so focused on sports I never thought about who I was outside of being an athlete and playing sports. It took me a long time to even find out what the next steps in my life were. I was living in Houston on my own and working for an MLM company barely making ends meet. My rent was $650 a month which I could barely pay. I had to ask my mom for money every other month so I wouldn't get kicked out. I asked God to open a door for me every night. I had faith that he was going to make something happen for me and once again he delivered. My best friend, and one of my roommates in Junior College, Metise Moore, got my foot in the door working as a Sales Consultant for Intuit. I told myself that I would take that opportunity and run with it! Working for Intuit, put me in a position to start my own business helping student-athletes reach their dreams. This is why it is important to have faith in yourself, your support system, and most importantly God. Days might seem dark but they won't stay that way forever.

Becoming a Student Athlete

Student-athletes are defined as students who participate in organized sports for the educational institution that they are enrolled in. I like to consider student- athletes as full-time students and full-time athletes. You cannot be a student- athlete if you are missing the student side. Colleges reward student-athletes for being great in both aspects with full scholarships or partial scholarships that will help cover the expenses of college. This is super important because college is EXPENSIVE! I want to give you this information so that you are able to set yourself up for success. Hopefully, this information will help you minimize as much debt as possible when you are starting out your adult life. The reality of life is that college is not free. In this section, I will break down how you can become a better student- athlete into 3 major categories: What you do to become a better person; what you do in the classroom to become a better student; and what you should be doing when you're participating in your sport to become a better athlete.

Athletes and parents of athletes - it is important that you put this information to work!

ARE YOU BECOMING A BETTER PERSON

When it comes to getting recruited, many athletes overlook becoming a better person. A great way to measure who you are as a person is by performing a self-evaluation. You have to look at yourself in the mirror and be honest with who you are. If your athletic ability was taken away today, who would you be? You might be able to lie to other people but you can't lie to yourself. You're the only person who knows if you are being honest with yourself. You need to evaluate your character and your integrity. Your character and integrity can be easily described as what you do when no one is looking. Many student-athletes fall into the trap of being labeled as a "jock." A jock is someone who is not humble and who thinks they are above everyone else. Jocks often have bad character and integrity. Your character & integrity is made up of how responsible you are, how respectful you are, how caring you are, how trustworthy you are, and what you do in the community. You do not want to be labeled as someone who is a jock or someone who has a bad character because once you develop this reputation it is very hard to get rid of it. You want to work on developing your character as early as possible.

Parents - make sure you are holding your child accountable. You want to work with them on being humble especially when they achieve great things. It is also important to celebrate all victories no matter how big or small. If you can find a balance between being humble and being confident, you will be very successful. It is important to remember that someone is always watching what you do, even when you think they are not. If you are not doing the right things, you want to work to improve this immediately. As you start going through the recruiting process coaches will ask your teachers, coaches, trainers, and family members about who you are as a person. Coaches are investing their livelihood in you so they will "cross every I and dot every T" to make sure you will be an asset to their program. Train your character and integrity: It will take you a long way in life.

IN THE CLASSROOM

The first thing a college coach looks for when they start recruiting an athlete is how well they are performing in the classroom. Coaches won't even think about taking a look at you if you are not performing well in the classroom. You want to make sure you are putting in the same amount of work off the field, as on the field. I know some of you are thinking things like: "it's too hard" or "my teacher doesn't like me" or "I get distracted too easily." I know these are some of your thoughts because I used to be in the same position. You have to be willing to try really hard and apply yourself. If you can't figure out the material on your own then ask for help. Many of my peers let their egos get the best of them because they were too proud to ask for help. This ultimately led to their downfall as a student. Don't be too proud to ask for help or ask for some guidance. In my experience teachers will reward you for putting in the effort and asking for help more times than not. If you were on the field in a game or on the court playing defense you wouldn't give up, so don't give up in the classroom, push yourself.

I'm a very competitive person, I hate to lose in anything that I participate in. I used this competitive mindset to help me approach the classroom. While in the classroom, I was going to compete to be the best student in the class. I was going to be the kid who knew the most information. Try adopting this method in your own life, and let me know how it works for you. Parents - keep an eye on how your child is performing in school. Stay on top of their tests and make sure they are bringing you their report cards.

Another thing you want to do as a student-athlete is choose a major or have some sort of idea of what direction you want to go as far as your studies. A lot of student-athletes don't think about what they want to do once they stop playing sports. Let me tell you, the harsh reality is everyone stops playing at some point in their life. You want to have something that you enjoy to fall back on once your athletic career is over. It is important to pick something you can see yourself doing in the future. This could be Criminal Justice, Engineering, Law School, etc.
Picking a major is also important because this helps you target the schools that you want to contact. This also helps you narrow down the process of choosing schools you want to apply for when you start getting recruited. This can also help you plan out what elective courses you want to take in high school to prepare you for your major.

Here's how you can make sure you are staying on track to graduate:

Freshman- ask your counselor for a list of your high school's NCAA core courses to make sure you are enrolled in the correct courses.

Sophomores - Register with the NCAA Eligibility Center.

Juniors - Check with your counselor to make sure you will graduate on time, and you are on track to complete the required amount of NCAA core courses. Take the ACT or SAT and submit your scores to the NCAA. At the end of the year, ask your counselor to upload your official transcript to the NCAA Eligibility Center.

Seniors - Finish taking your last NCAA core courses. Take the ACT or SAT again, if you need to. Make sure you submit your scores to the NCAA. Complete your academic and amateurism questions in your NCAA Eligibility Center account. After you graduate, ask your counselor to submit your final official transcript with your graduation date on it to the NCAA Eligibility Center.

You want to make sure that you are maintaining a high Core GPA (grade point average) throughout high school. The GPA scale is out of 4 points. I recommend maintaining at least a 3.0 + GPA, with a minimum of 2.8. Certain schools will require you to have a certain level GPA in order to be accepted into that school. You don't want to run into a problem where a coach wants to offer you a scholarship but he can't because you won't be accepted into the school. You also don't want to run into a problem where they already offered you a scholarship and you want to sign but weren't accepted into the school. On the flip side, having a high GPA can help you stand out from the competition. For example, if a coach is trying to decide between you and another recruit, and both of you are excellent players on the field but your competition has a 2.7 GPA and you have a 3.2 GPA the coach might be more inclined to choose you over the competition because you are less of a liability in the classroom. I remember one coach specifically telling me that he chose me because he knew I wouldn't be a problem in the classroom.

I know you hear that academics are important from everyone around you. It really is that important. Knowledge is power. No one can ever take your education away from you, and it helps you earn more money to pay for your education. Take care of your grades, Athletes, you are always a student first!

Participating In Your sport

The last piece to becoming the best recruit you can be is: what you are doing to become a better athlete while participating in your sport. Like I pointed out earlier, you want to adopt the idea of having a student mentality. This means applying a learning mindset to everything you do within your sport. You have to be willing to grow and adapt to the different aspects of your sport to get to the next level. If you are in a film session, make sure that you are taking good notes and asking questions if you don't understand. If you are in the weight room, follow specific instructions and listen to why you are doing that specific exercise. If you are at home, listen to podcasts & watch highlights of professionals who play/played your position. You can also watch instructional videos on how to become better at that position. You should ask your coaches and your trainers questions to gain a better understanding of what you should be working on to improve. This will translate into your play! You have to be obsessed with the grind! These are all things that I did in my sport to become the best athlete possible.

Becoming a great student-athlete requires you to put in the extra work. There's an old saying, "the amount of work you put in while no one is watching is what makes the great ones great". One of the sayings I live by is, "hard work beats talent when talent doesn't work hard." You can have all the talent in the world but a person who outworks you will win 9 out of 10 times. If you watch interviews of the most successful athletes, they talk about how hard they worked. Take Kobe Bryant for example. Kobe was known for his success as an NBA player but he is mostly known for his "Mamba Mentality" throughout all sports. Mamba mentality adopts the idea that no matter how good you are, how much taller you are, you will not be better than me because you will not outwork me. Everybody can put in the required amount of work but who's willing to go the extra mile to outwork the next man or woman? For example, you might need to show up before and stay after practice to work on your skills. You might need to get your teammates together without the coaches and work on your game. You might need to watch the film at home or even little things like doing pushups and sit-ups every morning & night. I remember my dad specifically taking me to the field or taking me to personal training sessions while my friends were going out to run the streets. I didn't understand it at the time, but when I started to receive outstanding accolades I knew why. When I got my first scholarship offer, I understood exactly why he pushed me to put extra work in. I want you to have that same feeling.

Another important factor that goes into becoming a better student-athlete while participating in your sport is becoming a captain, a leader, and a great teammate. Being a captain on your team is the ultimate achievement besides winning a championship. College coaches look for student-athletes who are captains on their team because they are normally someone who exemplifies what it means to be a leader (and they are voted on by the team). A captain is also someone who works harder than everyone else and they also hold others accountable. This is not something that is necessary but it is something you want to strive to achieve. This will make you stand out to a college coach. As a Quarterback, I was forced to become a leader and it wasn't easy. Back in those days, I was an introvert. I didn't like speaking in public or speaking in front of the team. For the most part, I was a quiet leader. I had to find my own leadership style, and I encourage you to find yours. You don't always have to be the most vocal leader, you can lead by example.

Lastly, find a balance between working, resting, and rewards. Learn how to balance the extra work with rest and other activities to reward yourself for the work you're putting in. You don't want to overwork yourself or give yourself too much praise. Try to find a good balance between the two. Make sure you are putting time into your recovery process. Take ice baths, stretch at night and after workouts, make sure you get treatment, and most importantly SLEEP! If you truly want to be successful as an athlete you're going to have to put down those video games!

How To Get Noticed

Gaining exposure and getting noticed is the first step of the recruiting process. It is also the most important for the simple fact that without exposure, coaches won't ever know who you are. If coaches don't know you are they will not be able to evaluate & recruit you. Getting coaches to notice you can be difficult if you aren't proactive. As I went through the recruiting process in high school, my father stayed on me about reaching out to coaches every week. This made me stay proactive in my own recruiting process. My father also reminded me that if I wanted to make it to the next level I had to stay committed to the grind. He made sure that I was at every camp possible. Every weekend he took me to a different camp to make sure I maximized my opportunities! My dad was just as committed to my future as I was and I truly appreciate him for that.

In this section, I have outlined how to gain exposure and how to get noticed by coaches. This information helped me gain over 20+ scholarship offers and get noticed by 100s of college coaches. This information will only work if you do. Make sure you are taking this information and applying it. Don't give up if it doesn't work the first couple of times, stay consistent and persistent and I promise it will work.

Committing To The Grind!

Getting noticed comes down to how committed you are. You have to be committed to getting better at every aspect of your life. You have to be committed to grinding to better your skills. You need to be the best in your specific sport and you have to be committed to outworking everyone. You have to outwork your teammates, all the student-athletes in your state and in the country. I advise athletes to always have the mindset that somebody is working when you aren't. This helps student-athletes focus on putting in extra work in the weight room, studying the game, and even spending extra time with their coaches going over how they can improve. Your grind has to be annoying! When I say your grind has to be annoying your parents have to be annoyed with how much you want to get better. Your friends need to be asking where you have been. You have to want to succeed as much as you want to live. This is how you become truly successful. IT HAS TO WORK OR IT HAS TO WORK!

Parents - if we're asking your children to be committed to their future, I have to ask you to be committed to their future as well. This means investing in your child's future. Too many student-athletes miss out on the opportunity to go to college or get their education paid for because they don't have the proper guidance. I am not saying this to say you are a bad parent. You have to learn the recruiting process yourself before you are able to educate your child. If you don't have time to learn the process, please make sure you are putting your child in touch with someone who can provide them with the information. This could be a mentor and coach like myself, or it could be a personal trainer - there are many options. Parents - you have to be willing to give up free time to commit to your child's future. This may mean taking them to extra training sessions when you get off of work. This may also mean taking them to camps or to college visits on the weekends. You have to put your child in the environment they wish to reach in order for them to thrive.

The same thing goes for life in general. You need to go test drive your dream car so you know what it feels like to drive it. After driving that car, you are willing to do anything to put yourself in a position to own that car. It's all about mentality.

Committing to your child's future may also mean investing money. The truth is many of the nation's top athletes have personal trainers, recruiting coaches, diets that they follow, and many other things that their parents have invested in to make sure that they succeed. You can decide which of these things you want to invest in if any, but these things do give your child an advantage in the recruiting process. Young student-athletes can't do it on their own they need your help!

FILM! FILM! FILM!

The best way to get noticed is by creating an effective highlight tape and getting it into the hands of college coaches. This plays a crucial part in helping them evaluate your talent level. There are a few different types of films you want to create for coaches to evaluate.

Highlight Tape - A highlight tape is a video that is composed of all of your best plays. Highlight tapes should showcase your talent in clips. They should start off with your most exciting and explosive plays. Highlight tapes should be between 2 and 6 minutes. The purpose of the highlight tape is to give coaches a quick insight into your talent level and to get them interested in you. Make sure that your highlight tape shows your versatility! Coaches don't want to see you do the same things over and over, they want to see how many different things you do well. This is how most coaches determine if they want to start recruiting you. If a coach likes your highlight tape he may request full game footage from you or your coach. This is why you want to play as hard as you can. A coach might also invite you to a camp to see you compete in person. You want to stay ready so you don't have to get ready.

Game Film - After you create your highlight tape and send it to coaches you should begin to receive feedback. Normally if a coach likes your highlight film he will request a full game film. A full game film is the entire recording of a game. In the film, they want to know how hard you play, how you react when things aren't going your way, and if you can play at a high level throughout the whole game. Make sure you aren't loafing and you go hard every play! They are watching.

Workout videos - Workout videos are a good way to keep coaches updated on your progress. You want to post these videos on your social media accounts. You also want to post these videos on your recruiting profiles. Any time you workout record it!

Videos from camps - Whenever you go to camps you want to make sure somebody is recording if possible.

That way you can follow the same process as workout videos. In some cases, these videos work better than the workout videos because it shows you competing against of athletes.

Go to Camps!

Another great way to get noticed is by going to camps. Whether you get invited to camps by coaches or you take it upon yourself to go to camps, this is a great way to meet coaches and get noticed. Camps normally have many college coaches running the drills and also looking for new prospects. This is a great way for both coaches and student-athletes to connect. This is the best way for athletes from small schools to get noticed. This was one of the main methods I used to gain exposure during my recruiting process. My father invested a lot of time and money into getting me to these camps. My father put me in development camps that helped me gain skills and knowledge that others didn't have. My dad also put me in camps that required me to compete against my peers. My father also made it possible for me to go to camps held by specific colleges. These camps helped me get noticed and get on the recruiting board of many coaches.

Not only do you want to go to these camps but you want to perform well. That's why it is imperative that you are putting in the extra work to get better. At most of the camps I went to, I finished in the top 2-3 Quarterbacks. This allowed me to gain huge exposure and put me on the radar of coaches. Some camps cost money and others are free. The key is investing in the correct camps that will maximize your child's exposure. Below I outline some camps that I want you to consider going to:

College Camps - College camps are a great way to introduce yourself to coaches. College coaches will invite you to these camps if they have seen your highlight tape and are interested, or you can register for these camps yourself. There's a lot of teaching, instruction, and competing at these camps. If you have a specific school you are interested in, make sure you go to those camps. **Examples** of these camps are the University of Maryland Camp, University Of Delaware Football Camp, Prairie View A&M University basketball camp. The camp dates will be posted on the school's athletic website. Most all schools have camps.

Combines - Combines are normally skilled-based camps that will require you to use your skills. These camps will have different tests depending on your sport. These tests normally test your running ability, your jumping ability, your strength, and your skills in your specific sport. **Examples :** **Football**: 40-yard dash, 5 10 5 shuttle. **Basketball**: vertical leap & lane drill.

Making sure you are going to the correct combines and you perform well is very important. These results are reported on your recruiting profile. This is also a great way for you to maximize exposure because the information is automatically sent to college coaches for evaluation. **Examples of**

combines: Rivals showcase, LBJ Skills camp, Under Armour skills camp. You can find these on google for your area.

Developmental Camps - These camps specialize in teaching student-athletes specific skills, giving knowledge, and providing instruction. These camps are helpful because they are normally run by retired professionals who are looking to share their knowledge and give back. **Examples:** Football University or FBU, Basketball Skills Camps. You can find these camps on google.

Contacting Coaches

Being proactive in your recruiting process by reaching out to coaches helps you gain exposure and get noticed. You don't want to wait for coaches to start contacting you, you want to get your name on their recruiting board as soon as possible. Once your sport's contact period begins, be sure to follow up communications with a phone call. Athletes can also initiate communication by either emailing or direct messaging coaches of programs they are interested in as early as possible. You want to send them your athletic recruiting profile or resume, which should include:

Your highlight video
Any sport-specific stats
Your Grades and GPA
Why you are interested in their school

This helps you get on the coach's radar before the contact period. Once the contact period rolls around, you will be one step ahead of the game. Make sure you are following up with a phone call. A lot of athletes get missed because they think that they aren't supposed to reach out to coaches or that their HS coach is doing it for them. I want you to stop having that mindset. You want to be the driver of your own recruiting process, not the passenger! When I was going through the recruiting process, I contacted at least 10-15 coaches a day. I was going to go get my scholarship, I didn't wait on anybody to give me a scholarship. I went and earned it. Below I have outlined the different ways you can contact coaches:

Social Media - Social media is a great way to reach out to coaches. I would say this is the best way to contact coaches. You want to reach out to coaches to introduce yourself and also share your highlight tape with them. Make sure you are following these coaches, DM'ing these coaches, and also dropping your tape under any post they have. You have to want it more than everyone else. Also, try to be different by adding emojis and BOLD text to your post and DMs. Coaches are very active on social media and always looking for new recruits across the different social media platforms. If you don't have these social sites you want to create them and start being active.

Twitter

Instagram

Facebook

LinkedIn

You also want to make sure that your social media page is clean. There should be no explicit content, and nobody should be posting disrespectful things on your pages. You also want to watch your language and make sure you are being respectful. You should post content that shows you are interested in getting to the next level. I used this information to gain over 15+ SCHOLARSHIP OFFERS through social media. Make sure you have your sport, height, weight, accomplishments, etc. in your bio so coaches can easily identify you! I lost a few scholarships because my social media accounts weren't clean. Coaches will go in the past to look at your post. A few coaches went 7 years back on my Twitter to see what types of things I was posting. I had some things on there that weren't appropriate and I lost a few scholarships offers because of that. Luckily, I had more to fall back on. A lot of kids aren't as fortunate as I was so don't get caught in that same position.

Emails - Emailing is another very effective way to get noticed. College coaches check their emails several times throughout the day. This is a great way to get their eyes on your highlight tape or introduce yourself. You want to make sure you are following up on your email because coaches get hundreds of emails each day. You want to create clear emails that have subject lines that grab the attention of the coach. If you can create subject lines that will grab the coach's attention, you will give yourself the best chance that the coaches will open the email, read the email and respond to your emails. Make sure you are including a personalized video in your email. Try to add a picture in the header, and whatever else that you can come up with. You have to be different and stand out!

Phones Calls - A well-placed phone call can be one of the most impactful ways to get your name on coaches recruiting boards. In fact, when going through my own recruiting process coaches used to tell me that for some reason recruits use this way to contact coaches the least. Taking the time to personally call the coaches is a great opportunity to set yourself apart from the competition. The best time to start calling college coaches is after you've sent them a couple of introductory emails. The NCAA recruiting rules state that D1 and D2 coaches aren't allowed to answer or return the call until June 15 after an athlete's sophomore year or September 1 of their junior year, depending on your sport. Keep this in mind as you're calling college coaches. Even if the coach isn't able to call you yet, they are still going to be building out their recruiting class by evaluating prospects online and at events. So leave a voicemail! The best time to contact coaches is at night time and on weekends.

There are a few steps I want you to take when contacting coaches.
First, I want you to send an introduction email or DM introducing yourself.
You then want to follow the email or DM with a phone call. These first two
steps should get you on the coach's radar, and they will start sending you
recruiting letters. You want to make sure that you are responding to those
recruiting letters. Lastly, I want you to keep in touch with these coaches. I
want you to make sure your name is always on the top of coaches' minds.
Don't stop reaching out to coaches until they tell you they aren't interested
anymore. You can find coaches' information by going to google and
searching the school you are interested in, plus the staff directory.

1. Send an introduction to coaches: This is your chance to introduce
yourself to college coaches. You want to send them an email or direct
message on social media introducing yourself, attaching your personalized
recruiting video/recruiting profile and you want the subject line to be
catchy.

2. Follow-up with a phone call: Once the contact period starts you want to
follow up your emails and direct messages with phone calls. D1 coaches
are not allowed to talk to you before the contact period so don't waste your
time calling these D1 coaches early.

3. Respond to letters from coaches: Although most communication will be
done through digital methods, coaches may send you recruiting letters. You
should respond to every recruiting letter that you receive from coaches
with either an email, text, or phone call.

4. Keep in touch with coaches and update them on your progress: You want
to reach out to coaches to update them on new stats or how you did in your
last game. If you are planning on visiting their school let them know you
want to set up a meeting with their coaching staff. If you have a
competition coming up soon invite them to come out and watch you play.

Coaches will communicate with you in various ways. Coaches rely on
mass emails, personal emails, personal letters, phone calls, camp invites,
questionnaires, and social media messages to communicate with recruits.
Depending on the method they use to contact, you will be able to tell
where you are on their recruiting board. Below I will outline each method
coaches will use and how you should respond:

Mass Emails - Coaches will send out a mass email to see which student-
athletes will respond. If you don't respond to these emails a coach may
think you are not interested and stop contacting you. You want to create a
response that you can use to reply to these types of emails. You want to

leave a good impression on coaches, even if you are not interested in that university. You should respond to the coach directly if you are interested.

Personal Emails - If you are getting personal emails from a coach this means you have passed the initial evaluation. Coaches use personal emails to show how interested they are in a recruit. While this email does not guarantee an offer, it is a good sign. These emails will have their signature on the email. It is important to check your email daily so that you can respond to these emails quickly. You want to answer any questions the coaches ask in the emails clearly. You also want to include your upcoming schedule as well.

Personal Letters - When you receive a handwritten letter signed by the coach, this means you are one of their top targets. You want to continue to reach out to these coaches to build a better relationship. You can either send your own handwritten letter back to the coaches or you can follow up with a phone call thanking them for the letter and also showing your interest. When I was going through the recruiting process I kept a shoebox of personal letters from coaches. My mom still has that shoebox to this day.

Phone Calls - A coach will schedule phone calls with athletes they are very interested in. During these conversations, you will build a relationship with these coaches. When prepping for the call do some research on the school. You should have questions that you want to be answered about the program. You also should be prepared to answer questions the coach might ask you. In my coaching program, we provide role-plays and scripts for you to use. You also can practice with a family member. Once you and the coach are done speaking, you always want to follow up with an email thanking the coach for their time. If you enjoyed the conversation you should include that as well. If the coach asked for any specific pieces of information make sure you include that in your follow-up email.

Camp Invitations - If the coach has you on their recruiting list they will send you camp invites. This might be a personal invite or it could also be generic. These camps are key to impressing the coaching staff. If you are interested in that particular school you should talk with your parents about attending the camp. If you are going to attend the camp send the coach an email letting them know you will be attending and you look forward to meeting them in person. The only thing left to do now is to show out!

Questionnaires - This will be the first piece of mail you will receive from coaches. These forms are used by coaches to build a list of recruits. If you are interested in the program fill the questionnaire out. If you are very interested in that program you should contact the coach and let them know that you are interested and let them know you filled out the questionnaire.

You want to start preparing to talk to coaches by gathering all of the information you will need to communicate with them. You want to have a recruiting profile where all of your information is kept. You always want to have a centralized link that coaches can click to access your information. This is very important because coaches are always on the go, they don't have time to go searching for all of your information. It makes you stand out if you make this easy for them. Below I have outlined some of the key information you will need to include on your recruiting profile:

Stats - Your best athletic stats, should be verified, you can also include stats from combines or times from camps.
Highlight tape - You always want to include your highlight tape or workout videos.

Academic Information - Your ACT/SAT scores and GPA.
Contact Information - Your phone number, email, coach's phone number, or personal trainer's phone number.
Schedule - When and where you will be competing during the season.

How to find coaches' information: To find the coach's contact information you can go to the university's athletic website and search the staff directory. You want to contact the recruiting coordinator or someone on the recruiting staff. You also want to contact your position coach or the assistant coach. You rarely want to send an email to the head coach initially. You want to be committed to this process because it will take some time. You want to set out some time every week to do this. This is also why it's important, to be honest with your talent level and what level you want to play to maximize your time.

What to ask coaches: When preparing to communicate with coaches you want to come up with four different types of questions. You want to come up with academic questions, athletic questions, cultural questions, and financial questions. An academic question might be "what are your most common majors on the team?" An athletic question could be "How would you prefer I share my updates with you?" A cultural question may be "what is the housing situation for athletes?" A financial question might be "Does the program have scholarships available?" We go over what questions are essential to your success in my coaching program.

Questions coaches will ask: Coaches will ask questions sort of like a job interview. These coaches want to learn more about you and your personality. I hated talking to coaches when I first got on the phone but I grew to enjoy it after practicing using role plays. You get better at speaking with coaches the more you talk to them. I like to tell athletes experience is the best teacher. Some questions coaches might ask you:

How's your season going?

Why do you think you can play at this level?

What are you looking for in a program?

What are your GPA and test scores?

What schools are you talking to?

Parents - While you and your child are going through the recruiting process it is important that you are invested in your child's future. This means supporting them to the best of your ability. This doesn't mean you should be doing the work for them. Student-athletes should be contacting coaches, not their parents. College coaches are recruiting athletes. They are not recruiting the parents. At the beginning of the process, it is imperative that you let coaches get to know your child. All forms of communication should come from the child. This will show that the student-athlete is responsible enough to handle their recruiting process, while also getting to know them personally. Parents should always help their children if they don't know what to say or if they are extremely shy. You can practice with them by conducting role-plays. We also provide professional role-plays in my coaching program.

Parents - if you have questions, you should send them through your child. Parents - you can start to ask questions when you and your child start taking official and unofficial visits. If you are having real problems with your child reaching out to coaches then you can take measures to reach out yourself. It is better if you reach out than not reaching out at all.

At the end of the recruiting process when you start to receive offers, the conversations start to be more about the financials. At this time parents should start taking over the conversations. In my coaching program, I teach you how to negotiate your scholarship offers.

Key Elements of the Recruiting Process

There are a few different elements of the recruiting process that parents and student-athletes must understand in order to be successful. In this section, we will go over those key elements. Make sure you are taking notes so that you fully understand these elements. We will be covering how to make sure you are eligible academically. We will go over the different contact periods and timelines. We will also talk about the different types of visits, scholarships, and letters. Lastly, I will make sure you understand the application process and how to pick the right school that fits your goals and dreams.

Academic Eligibility

The most important aspect I want to make sure you understand is the academic eligibility requirements. This is often the most overlooked aspect for families who aren't sure about the recruiting process. The eligibility requirements vary from NCAA, JUCO, and NAIA schools. Different schools will also have their own requirements for you to gain entrance to their school. This is why it is important to stay on top of your grades and maintain a high GPA and core GPA. You also want to make sure you are preparing for the SAT or the ACT. These are standardized tests that you have to take. Your GPA and test scores can also determine if a coach chooses you over another recruit. Coaches will be investing a lot of time and money into their recruits so they want to make sure that they don't have to worry about you academically when you arrive on campus. Staying on top of your grades will set you up for more scholarship opportunities academically and athletically. You want to be an asset, not a liability.

Your freshman year of high school is the time to start thinking about your eligibility. This is especially important if you are looking to play Division I or Division II. Focusing on your eligibility allows you to stay on track to complete your core courses. In my situation, once it became apparent that I wanted to pursue this dream, my support system made sure that I was on top of all the requirements. My dad made sure that I was studying material that was going to prepare me for the ACT/SAT. My guidance counselor also made sure that I was maintaining a high GPA and taking all of my core courses.

When you are setting goals for your dreams, you want to make sure you include academic goals for yourself as well. I advise most of the athletes I speak with to set goals around following the Division I & Division II requirements because if you can meet those standards you will be eligible for all other levels. It is important to also note what types of school you are targeting so that you understand what their requirements are to gain entrance. Just because you meet the academic requirements to play in that division, you might not meet the school's requirements to gain entrance. This is why it is important, to be honest with yourself to know exactly what schools you are targeting.

Becoming NCAA Eligible

If you are interested in playing at the DI, DII, or DIII level then you'll need to create an NCAA Certification Account. Once you sign up and complete the registration for the account, the NCAA will assess your eligibility through it. The Certification account costs money but there are also fee waiver options available for athletes who are financially challenged. You also want to make sure you are meeting with your guidance counselor. I can remember vividly meeting with my guidance counselor at least two times a year. Once at the beginning of the year to make sure that I was taking the correct core courses. I also met with her once at the end of the year to make sure I was still on track to complete these core courses. Meeting with my counselor helped me stay focused on doing the best I could in the classroom to set myself apart. Below I will outline the key elements to gaining NCAA eligibility for DI and DII student-athletes

:

GPA (Core Courses) - The NCAA only uses the GPA of your core courses to determine your eligibility. This means that courses that are electives, like a weight training class or a drama class don't count against you. These courses don't go into determining your NCAA eligibility, so if you take a course like this and have trouble there is no need to panic. On the flip side, you can not afford to fail a core course. For Division I athletes the minimum GPA is 2.3 on a 4.0 scale. For DII athletes the minimum is 2.0. You should meet with your guidance counselor to make sure that you are on track. The NCAA also provides a core course worksheet as a resource. We cover this topic more in-depth in my coaching program.

Core Courses - All student-athletes are required to complete 16 core courses in high school. These courses vary from math, social sciences, English, and physical science classes. It is important to speak with your guidance counselor because each school has a list of approved Core Courses to choose from. It is important to stay on track to complete these courses. You are required to complete 10 of these core courses by the end of your junior year. There is a slight difference in becoming eligible for DII, and DIII schools but if you complete the requirements for DI, then you will be eligible for all other levels.

NCAA Sliding Scale - The NCAA will use a combination of your SAT, ACT, and GPA scores to determine if you're eligible. Athletes who have a lower GPA can still become NCAA eligible if they can meet the ACT/SAT requirement outlined on the sliding scale. This means if you have a high core GPA then you can qualify with a lower SAT/ACT score. If you have a lower core GPA, you will need a higher score to qualify.

ACT/SAT - The minimum SAT score for DI eligibility is 900. The minimum score for the ACT is a 75 sum score. To be eligible to play at the DII level you must receive a 70 ACT or 840 SAT. The NCAA defines the sum score as the combined scores of the following four sections: English, mathematics, reading, and science. You can also take the ACT and SAT multiple times. If you do this you can use your best score in each category to create your best sum score.

D3 - Division III schools are responsible for their own eligibility rules. You can hold off on creating an NCAA Certification account because they will not review your eligibility. You can always create a free NCAA Profile Page and upgrade later if you need to.

Junior College - The requirements are simple for Junior Colleges. All you need to do is graduate high school, and earn your standard academic diploma. You can also complete your GED, and become eligible for junior college.

The Recruiting Calendar

The recruiting calendar is used to stay on top of the NCAA Recruiting Rules and understand the important dates in the recruiting process. It is important to understand these rules and timelines to make sure that you are not violating any key rules. The NCAA recruiting calendar shows the dates throughout the year when coaches can be in contact with recruits. This was one of the things my dad kept on me constantly about. Knowing these dates will help you come up with an effective strategy to maximize the recruiting process. The most important dates are going to be June 15, going into the athlete's junior year, or September 1, depending on what sport you play. This is when coaches can start responding and reaching out to athletes.

There are key periods of the NCAA Recruiting Calendar that you want to understand. Those periods are the evaluation period, the contact period, the dead period, and the quiet period. Below I will outline and go over some key components of each period:

Evaluation Period - The Evaluation period is the time of the year when coaches can visit high schools or watch the recruit compete. During this period coaches can not communicate with the recruit or parents off the college campus. Coaches will visit the school to speak with the teachers, the guidance counselor, and coaches to evaluate the character of the recruit. This is why it is important to develop your character & integrity which I touched on earlier. The evaluation period is also the time where coaches will watching practices, games and speak with coaches. It will give the coach a sense of how hard the athlete works, his leadership, and how he acts around his teammates. While coaches aren't allowed to talk to recruits off college campus they are still able to call, text, direct message, and email athletes.

Parents it is important that you let your child speak with the coach as much as possible. There is a time and place where the coaches will want to speak with the parents but this time is for the athletes. At this point, the coach has already watched your highlight tape and checked on your eligibility. In my coaching program, I provide role plays for the student-athletes. I also provide resources on what to expect and how to prepare for during this period. This period is very specific, not all sports have this period. These sports allow an evaluation period:

1.DI Football (FBS and FCS),

2.DI Men's/Women's Basketball

 3.DI Women's Volleyball
4.DI Softball
5.DII Football
6.DII Men's/Women's Basketball

You can find specific dates online and we also cover them in my recruiting coaching program

Contact Period - The Contact period is when coaches can use all forms of communication to communicate with the recruit. Coaches can call, text, email, and direct message the athletes. Coaches can also have in-person contact with the recruit on the college campus, at the athlete's homes or school, and also at tournaments.

I will never forget the first time I met Coach Johnson from Marist College. I was on the way to the bathroom from my English class when he stopped me and asked if I knew where Coach Brooks' class was located. Of course, I knew where the class was so I offered to take him there. On the way to the classroom we were talking and I ended up asking who he was there to see. He said I'm here to speak with LaVell McCullers and the rest is history. If I didn't know what dates coaches might visit the school, I wouldn't have been prepared to speak with Coach Johnson when we bumped into each other.

I wanted to tell you that story to remind you to always stay ready. When you understand these dates you begin to understand how you can prepare for these periods.

Parents - coaches use this time to get to know their top recruits as they start to offer scholarships. During this period coaches will schedule in-home visits with recruits and their families. This will allow the coaches to evaluate the recruit's personalities and figure out if they would be a good addition to the program. Parents - you want to step back a little during a home visit. This also gives recruits the opportunity to get to know a coach outside of the campus. During this time, parents and recruits can ask questions to understand more about the coaches and their program. If a coach does visit you during the contact period, this is a sign that you are high on their recruiting board. Some coaches use this time to give out scholarship offers but it's not guaranteed. You want to make sure you're prepared just in case. Get on the same page with your parents before the coach arrives.

You can find specific dates for your sport online and we go over how to prepare for the contact period in my coaching program.

Dead Period - The dead period is a period where coaches cannot have any in- person communication with the athletes. A lot of people think that all communications cut off during this period but it is important to understand that you can still communicate with coaches. You can still communicate with coaches through social media, phone calls, and text messages, and email as well. During this period you want to manage your time wisely. I encourage you to update your recruiting profile with your latest highlight tape, and recent transcripts. You also want to add your GPA, test scores, and any stats or accomplishments to your recruiting profile. I suggest you draft a new personal statement that shows coaches your character and also create a recruiting video that is personalized to each specific coach. You also want to research college rosters to find out if coaches are recruiting for your position. If they are recruiting your position, add these coaches to your target list and take virtual college tours. Use this time to connect with coaches on social media and email coaches. You also want to study for the ACT & SAT if possible. One of the most important things you don't want to forget is to maintain your workout schedule. Make sure you are putting in the extra work to become better. Be committed to your dreams and goals. Rest and recharge your minds and bodies. You don't want to become burnt out from overworking yourself. Find your balance. Parents use this time to plan unofficial visits, camps, and other things to help put their child in the college athlete environment.

Quiet Period - The Quiet period is the period when you can talk to coaches in person on their campus. Coaches are not allowed to watch athletes in person or visit their homes or schools. You can still text, call, direct message, or email coaches. You should also be proactively reaching out to coaches during this time. This period only applies to DI and DII schools. Use this period to go on unofficial visits because coaches cannot come to you. It's very easy to set up a visit.

You can find specific dates online and we go over how to prepare for the quiet period in my recruiting coaching program.

Visits

If you ask anyone who's been through the recruiting process, they will tell you that visits are the best part of the recruiting process. This was definitely the best time of my recruiting process. There are two types of visits: official and unofficial. When I was a freshman and sophomore my dad made sure to take me on unofficial visits. He wanted to put me in the environment of being a collegiate athlete. That played a huge part in me committing to getting to the next level. It also gave me the mindset that I needed to be able to get to the next level. Once I became a junior and senior I started taking official visits and it was one of the most fun experiences in my life. Both visits include going on campus tours, watching games, meeting the staff being on the field during warmups, and many more activities. This section will break down everything you need to know about visits:

Official Visits - You're probably wondering what makes a visit "official." The visit becomes official when any part of your visit is financed by the institution you are visiting. If you are invited on an official visit that means you are one of their top recruits and this is a huge step on your recruiting journey. It is important to be prepared for these visits.

Rules - Each division has its own rules on the topic of college visits. Division 1 has the most strict set of rules you must abide by. The NCAA only allows a recruit to take five visits to Division I schools, and you are limited to one per school. DII and DIII schools are also limited to one per school, but there is no limit on the total amount of visits a student-athlete can take. The university can pay for you and your parent's transportation to and from the campus, lodging for your visit, three meals per day, and three tickets to home sports events. Schools can only provide transportation for parents if they travel in the same car or plane as the recruit. Separate cars and plane tickets will have to be purchased on your own.

On all levels, the recruits can only take one official visit per school. Official visits may last up to 48 hours long, or over the span of a weekend. Universities can choose to finance your whole trip which is what happens in most cases, or they can choose to finance part of your trip if they don't have the money. There are specific dates and information we cover in my coaching program.

How It Works - You can start taking official visits your junior year for most sports and divisions. The coach will ask you to come on an official visit through social media messages, phone calls, emails, etc. Once a coach invites you on an official visit, consult with your parents to see what weekend would be the best for you all. Coaches will send you your flight information and coordinate the trip for you. You will be evaluated during this visit and most times you receive an official offer on these types of visits. Keep in mind this is not guaranteed though.

Parents - Universities are allowed to invite parents on official visits. Parents have a role throughout the official visit: Let the athlete be the focus. Parents should allow athletes to take control of the conversations and be the center of focus. You want to allow your child to form their own opinion about the school. Once the conversation turns from sports and the program to finances, and scholarships this is where you want to jump in.

What happens - Every visit will be a different experience but you can always expect to go on a tour of the campus. Coaches want to show you what campus life will be like and where you will be staying for 4 years. Make sure you are taking notes of what you liked and what you didn't. This will help you remember things from your visit. You will also meet a few of the team members and maybe spend a night with them. Coaches want to see if you and the other players have chemistry. One of the team members might take you through a workout. Staff members including coaches are not allowed to organize workouts. Sometimes visits will include locker room tours, tickets to a game, dinner with the coaches and family, and more.

Questions - On visits, you will spend some one on one time with the coaches that are recruiting you. This is a chance for you to ask questions that you have. Before the visit come up with questions and write them down so that you can ask the coaches. The coach will also want to ask you some questions as well. Some questions might be

What other schools are you getting recruited by?

What other visits have you been on?

When can you commit?

We cover what questions to ask & also what questions to expect in the coaching program.

What to wear - You want to look presentable on the visit. You can wear high school gear with some nice jeans and shoes. You also could wear a collared shirt with khakis. It's all up to how you want to appear. For women, you can wear a dress or nice slacks and jeans. You want to avoid wearing ripped jeans, hats, flip flops, and sweatpants. Bring athletic clothes and shoes in case you get invited to workout with the team. Also, bring a notepad and prepare some questions to ask coaches. Make sure you research the school as well.

Follow Up - After your visits you want to make sure you are following up with coaches. Send them a thank you note or a message letting them know how much you enjoyed your time. I can also let them know the next time you'll be competing if they want to come to watch in person. This keeps you at the top of their mind and some that you are being proactive.

Unofficial Visits - Unofficial visits are a great way for student-athletes to put themself in the environment of a college student-athlete. Due to the new rule change, student-athletes cannot go on unofficial visits coordinated by the athletic department until August 1 of the recruit junior year. Athletes can go on unofficial visits before August 1 of the recruits junior but they aren't allowed to have any conversations with any coaches. The best part about unofficial visits is the ability to take as many as you want. There is no limit to the amount you can take and there is no age limit.

What happens - Every visit is different. Because unofficial visits are normally arranged by parents it will be up to you how you spend your time. You may also be invited to attend a sports event. On your unofficial visit, you might want to visit the different housing options, hang out on the campus, and even eat in the cafeteria or food court. Make sure you are writing down your thoughts about the school.

Rules - On official visits, you are allowed to stay on campus with an enrolled student but there are more rules based on the division level. DI and DII schools the recruit must pay the rate for staying in the dorm. DIII recruits can stay in the dorms with the school financing the stay. The parents of the recruit have to find their own accommodations though.

Questions - On your official visit you want to ask a few questions to gain a better understanding of the program and school. Write these questions down and take them with you on the visit. Some questions you might want to ask are: "what are the requirements to get into this school?" " What is your coaching style?" " what are you looking for in a recruit?"
What to wear - You want to look presentable on the visit. You can wear high school gear with some nice jeans and shoes. You also could wear a collared shirt with khakis. It's all up to how to want to appear. For women, you can wear a dress or nice slacks and jeans. You want to avoid wearing ripped jeans, hats, flip flops, and sweatpants. Bring athletic clothes and

shoes in case you get invited to workout with the team. Also, bring a notepad and prepare some questions to ask coaches. Make sure you research the school as well.

Follow Up - After your visits you want to make sure you are following up with coaches. Send them a thank you note or a message letting them know how much you enjoyed your time. You can also let them know the next time you'll be competing, and ask if they want to come to watch in person. This keeps you at the top of their mind.

Scholarships

Scholarships are what every student-athlete strives to earn. Scholarships are what student-athletes earn to pay for college. When you go through the recruiting process, coaches will start to give out "offers." These offers refer to verbal scholarships. There are two different types of scholarships. The first is a full-ride scholarship that covers every college expense throughout your college career. The other is a partial scholarship that covers part of your college expenses. Athletic scholarships typically are one-year agreements but some can be multi-year. Athletic scholarships are offered by most DI, and DII schools. Athletic scholarships are also offered at the NAIA and NJCAA levels as well. It is important to note that most scholarships are not full rides. It depends on the headcount and what sport you are playing. It is important to note that headcount sports will only give full-ride scholarships. For men, these sports are DI basketball and DI-A football. For women, it is DI basketball, volleyball, gymnastics, and tennis. All other sports and division levels offer full and partial scholarships. That offer depends on what level recruit you are and how high you are on your coach's recruiting board.

How do I earn a full ride? - It is important to know that most student-athletes do not receive full-ride scholarships. Only about 1% of student-athletes receive full rides. Still, you should still strive to earn a full-ride scholarship because it is very possible. If you take the information I provided you on mentality and how to get noticed, you will put yourself in a position to earn a full scholarship. The only way I earned my full-ride scholarship is by changing my mindset. I was honest with myself about my talent level and about what level I could see myself playing. I was honest with myself about how much work I was willing to put in to earn a full-ride scholarship. Once I was able, to be honest with myself, I was able to commit to making sure I did everything in my power to earn that scholarship. I set clear and concise goals, and I put in the extra work on and off the field. Most importantly no matter what the coaches told me or what I went through, I had faith in myself, in God, and in my support system. In the end, I was able to earn a full-ride scholarship. Sometimes, moving down a division level will get you more money. A lower-level recruit for DI might receive a larger scholarship at the DII level. Be open-minded to all opportunities.

How do I know if I'm eligible to receive a scholarship? - In order to receive a scholarship to a DI or DII university you must meet the eligibility requirements. This means you must be up to date with your core courses and also maintaining the required GPA. You must also be considered an amateur athlete. An amateur athlete is someone who has NEVER been paid to participate in their sport. If you have been paid to participate you may be subject to ineligibility. It is also important to remember that just because you meet the requirements, doesn't mean you are going to receive a scholarship. Meeting these requirements increases your chances the better you are academically.

What happens when I receive an "offer?" - An "offer" refers to a verbal scholarship offer. A coach might extend a verbal offer anytime throughout the recruiting process. These offers are unofficial verbal contracts between a coach and athlete. These scholarship offers aren't set in stone until you sign your national letter of intent. You want to ask coaches if the offer is a full-ride offer or a partial scholarship. This is pivotal to choosing whom you are going to commit to. As a student-athlete, you can verbally commit to an offer at any point. Committing to a school can be a good thing and a bad thing. It is a good thing because committing to a popular school often influences more coaches to take a look at who you are. On the flip side, committing too early can put you at a disadvantage if you change your mind later.

When you receive a verbal offer you want to thank the coach and ask them if you can take some time to weigh out your options. During this time you also want to speak with your support system and think about taking an official visit to that school. You can commit to a program and you can also de-commit from a program. Just keep in mind doing this can make coaches think twice about recruiting you.

Can my scholarship be taken away? - The answer is yes. There are a few different situations where your scholarship might be taken away. Unfortunately, a coach might take your scholarship away if you are injured. Whether you are injured in practice or in a game your scholarship can be pulled depending on the severity of the injury. The other reason your scholarship offer might be pulled is if you aren't maintaining a good character. You want to make sure that you aren't getting in trouble in school, in the community, or at home. You want to make sure that you are maintaining a clean social media because once they offer you it is a representation of their program. I ran into a situation in my recruiting process where a coach pulled an offer from me. The coach went back and looked at my social media pictures from a couple of years prior. I had retweeted some pictures that did not reflect well on their program so he pulled my offer. I wasn't even aware of some of those pictures I had retweeted. Although it wasn't a reflection of the person I was growing to be, it still had a negative impact on my image of that particular coach. You want to make sure you are keeping a clean image so these situations do not happen to you.

Are there any other scholarships I can receive? - Most student-athletes aren't offered full-ride scholarships, because of this I encourage athletes to look into earning academic scholarships. There are some requirements that student-athletes need to meet to be eligible for academic scholarships. Most of the time you are required to have a high GPA and high test scores. DIII schools only offer academic scholarships so this might be something you want to look into. Academic scholarships are also more secure than athletic scholarships because they cannot be pulled if you are injured or because of poor performance. There are scholarships for almost anything out there. Literally anything! In my senior year, I won a motorcycle club scholarship. I used that scholarship money to buy a new laptop for college. You can search the web for types of scholarships from different corporations, nonprofit organizations, and private organizations. Make sure to fill out the Free Application for Federal Student Aid (FAFSA) as well. You could qualify to receive fed aid grants and loans.

The Application Process and Deadlines

At many points throughout the recruiting process, you may become overwhelmed and It is easy to forget about the application process. That is why I am here to help you. In my coaching program, I help you with the application process and applying to schools. If you are unorganized you can miss these important deadlines. There are seven parts to the application process. I have outlined these parts below:

1.**Registering for and taking the ACT and SAT:** If you are an underclassman you should be preparing to take your ACT/SAT. You can prepare by taking the PSAT and taking prep courses. By your junior year, you want to register and take both ACT and SAT. Registration usually opens up one month before the test date. You can take the SAT as many times as you want and you can take the ACT up to 12 times. I would recommend no more than 5 times. These things do cost money but there are fee waivers available for economically disadvantaged students. You can use these two times for each test.

2.**Registering with the NCAA Eligibility Center (for DI and DII) and/ or the NAIA Eligibility Center:** As we went over earlier you want to register for a Certification Account with the NCAA Eligibility Center if you plan on going to a D1 or D2 school. If you plan on going to an NAIA school you need to register with their Eligibility Center. If you are looking at playing on the DIII level you can create a profile page to stay up to date on important information. The NCAA Eligibility Center looks at your high school core courses, your core GPA, and your ACT/SAT test scores to determine eligibility. Your official scores have to be sent directly from the testing agencies, so use code "9999" for NCAA and "9876" for NAIA when you request those scores. It's important to register by your junior year so you can go on an official visit.

3. **Filling out and sending in college applications:** You should have your target list of schools you want to apply to narrow down by the end of summer leading into your senior year. This will give you enough time to apply to the schools that you want to go to. These applications cost money, that's why it's important to build a target list. There is no limit to how many schools you can apply too but it is time-consuming so be careful. Each university has different deadlines. Make sure you are marking these deadlines on your calendar to stay on top of them. You should consider the common application which allows you to send multiple schools the same application information.

4. **Submitting your FAFSA paperwork:** All students are eligible for financial aid. In order to receive this financial aid, you must complete the

Free Application for Federal Students. You will need to obtain your social security number, most recent tax returns, bank statements, and an FSA ID to sign electronically. Make sure you are keeping up with these deadlines because they are always changing.

5. Requesting your final amateurism certification: April 1 of your senior year you must request your final amateurism certificate if you plan on playing at the DI or DII level. Make sure you update your information in the NCAA Eligibility Center to become cleared to play at the college level.

6. Sending your final transcripts and proof of graduation to the Eligibility Center: You must prove to the NCAA that you graduated. You do this by sending in your final transcripts with your graduation date included. You can also have an administrator from your high school sign a proof of graduation and fax it in.

7. Signing the acceptance letter: Everything becomes official when you receive your acceptance letter and you accept to attend that university. Each school has its own deadlines so make sure you are noting when the deadline to accept is. The hard work is almost done!

Choosing The Right School

Now that you have multiple offers from universities you have a difficult decision to make. Not all offers are equal and you should take this into consideration when choosing your school. You want to compare your offers against each other to see which one makes the most sense for your future dreams. There are no correct answers but I can help you make the best decision. Below I have outlined some of the key elements that go into making your decision.

Examine your offers - Across the different divisions and the different sports, the scholarship amount varies. Most students strive to earn a full scholarship but in reality not many receive them. You want to figure out the time frame your coach wants you to accept the offer. You can always ask the coach for more time if you need it. Examine which schools are offering to cover the most cost of attendance.

Examine your schools - An important decision that you want to consider is the major that you want to study. This is important because not all schools offer the same majors. Some schools might offer your major and others might not. As you are building your target list you want to make sure the schools that you are adding have your major.

Think about location - The location of where you attend school is something that is very important to families. If you are a person who wants to stay close to home, narrow down your target list to the schools that are surrounding your location. If you want to venture out into the world, focus on the states you would like to spend 4 years living in.

Do you vibe with the coaches? - This is one of the most important factors in choosing the fit of the school. You will be spending the majority of your time with your coaches. You should want to make sure you have a good connection with your coaches. If you have a better connection with one coach over another this could be a key factor in your choice to attend that university.

Are you going to play? - You want to consider how much you will pay when you decide to attend that school. Coaches will offer you all types of playing time but you want to focus on the ones that don't. You want to focus on the coaches who tell you that you will have to work for your spot because these are the coaches that are going to give you a fair chance. You also want to research how many people they currently have in your position and when they are graduating. This will give you an idea of how many people you will have to compete against.

National Letter of Intent and National Signing Day

Now it's time to make it official. Everything becomes official when you sign your National Letter of Intent. Not all schools use the NLI and it is not mandatory. Many athletes throw signing parties on national signing day. You don't have to sign your NLI on the first day of the signing period but people who know where they are going normally do. Check with your specific sport for the dates of your signing period. If you miss the signing period it is not too late but it is unlikely there will be any roster spots left. When your student athlete receives their NLI document, the appropriate Signing Period should be checked. If the Signing Period has begun for their sport, they must sign within seven days of the issue date (noted on the document). If they receive the NLI document before the Signing Period window opens, they must wait until 7 a.m. on the first date of the period. The student athlete's parent or legal guardian must also sign the document. College coaches cannot be present during the signing.

National Letter of Intent - Signing your NLI means 3 things:

1. **You are committed to at least one year at that university.** You do not need to sign after the first time and the school is required to let the student-athlete know if they are renewing their scholarship.

2. **The school is promising you a scholarship for the upcoming year.** You will need to sign the financial aid package and your NLI.

3. **Your recruiting journey is complete.** You can not be recruited by any other schools. This is a legally binding contract. You want to make sure that you understand all aspects before signing. Your coach can help you with any questions or concerns when it comes to signing your NLI. While you have signed your NLI this does not mean you have been admitted to the university. You want to make sure you met all requirements to be enrolled.

NLI Release Rules - If you change your mind about attending the school you signed your NLI with you can ask the coaches to be released from the program. One reason why this happens is a school goes through a coaching change. Another reason is you weren't accepted into that school and you want to enroll in another school. The NLI is between the university and the athlete, not the coaches.

If you are a senior and you are still looking to get recruited it is not too late. However, you are behind the curve. You want to put everything I outlined in this book into overdrive. Unsigned seniors can still find opportunities because coaches are known to recruit well into the summer months looking to fill roster spots. You also might want to consider going to a prep school or junior college. In my coaching program, we cover how these are good alternative options.

Closing

By now, you understand what it takes to go from an unnoticed student-athlete to living out your dream of playing sports collegiately. As I share this information, I think about all of the past student-athletes that could have benefitted from this information. I want to challenge you to take action and apply this knowledge. A wise man once told me that knowledge isn't power, applied knowledge is power. If you don't apply the information given then you wasted your time learning this information. If you are committed to your grind and committed to bettering yourself as a person, doors will start to open up that you couldn't even imagine. You will go through some ups and downs during the recruiting process but don't give up. There will be times you feel like giving up but your breakthrough is on the other side of the struggle. I challenge you to stay committed to your future no matter what life throws at you. I challenge you to be honest with yourself. I challenge you to set goals and achieve them. I challenge you to have faith in yourself, in your support system, and God, and you will achieve all of your dreams and beyond.

I want to thank you again for taking the time to read my book. I hope you received some great value from it. As you move forward, stay connected with me and learn about the other resources I offer to help you navigate the recruiting process. If you would like 1-on-1 guidance through the recruiting process, please contact me at crossandcrownconsulting.com. Never give up on your goals and dreams. Keep in mind this information got me over 20+ scholarship offers and ultimately a full-ride scholarship. Keep growing and I expect to see you at the top!

The Recruiting Mentor,

LaVell McCullers

Made in the USA
Middletown, DE
07 May 2021